When Fish Got Feet Sharks Got Teeth, and Bugs Began to Swarm

A Cartoon Prehistory of Life Long Before Dinosaurs

WRITTEN AND ILLUSTRATED BY

HANNAH BONNER

NATIONAL GEOGRAPHIC

WASHINGTON, D.C.

For John T. Bonner, uncle extraordinaire and inspiration

ACKNOWLEDGMENTS

Six scientists kindly agreed to be my advisors and keep me on the straight and narrow, scientifically speaking. They were all exceptionally generous with their time and knowledge, and were true partners in shaping this book. John Beck, a geologist and fossil spore researcher at Weston Observatory of Boston College, helped me with the geological history and geography. Joanne Kluessendorf of the Weis Earth Science Museum in Wisconsin and her husband, Don Mikulic of the Illinois State Geological Survey, world experts on Silurian reefs, provided me with all the information and guidance necessary to recreate a reef and its inhabitants on pages 10–13. Carol Hotton, a paleobotanist with the National Museum of Natural History, guided me through the intricacies of prehistoric plant life. Cary Easterday at Northeastern Illinois University took care of terrestrial invertebrates—the bugs, in other words. And last but not least, Corwin Sullivan at the Harvard Museum of Natural History took a tremendous amount of time away from teaching and finishing his dissertation in order to help me with the vertebrates, which were many and tricky to show correctly.

I would also like to thank the following scientists whom I consulted via e-mail or in person: Tyler Keillor and Kaliope Monoyios for their help with reconstructing Tiktaalik, and Phillipe Janvier for help with the bony fish. My thanks also to Dennis Murphy, Eben Rose, Kirk Johnson, Bill DeMichele, John Maisey, Mary Parrish, Simon Braddy, and Pat Gensel.

Then there was turning all this science into a book worth reading: My editor, Marfé Ferguson Delano, was an angel, shepherding the text from rough beginnings to final story with patience and expertise. The designers at National Geographic were also terrific, with Ruthie Thompson in particular spending long hours getting the text and images to intertwine properly. Last but not least, my thanks to Nancy Laties Feresten, the mastermind and ongoing godmother of this series.

And finally, a huge thanks to my family and friends for their love, support, and feedback.

Book design by Hannah Bonner and Ruthie Thompson with David M. Seager, *Art Director*. The text is set in Gilgamesh medium.

Library of Congress Cataloging-in-Publication Data
Bonner, Hannah.
  When fish got feet, sharks got teeth, and bugs began to swarm: a cartoon prehistory of life long before dinosaurs / written and illustrated by Hannah Bonner.
     p. cm.
   ISBN 1-4263-0078-6 (hardcover)
   ISBN 1-4263-0079-4 (library binding)
  1. Paleontology—Paleozoic—Juvenile literature.   2. Paleontology—Devonian—Juvenile literature.   3. Paleontology—Silurian—Juvenile literature.   4. Fishes, Fossil—Miscellanea—Juvenile literature.   5. Prehistoric animals—Miscellanea—Juvenile literature.   I. Title.
  QE725.B67 2007
  560—dc22

                              2006020768

ISBN-13: 978-1-4263-0078-3 (HC); 978-1-4263-0079-0 (Library)

Printed in the United States of America

TABLE OF CONTENTS

What, you don't recognize Pennsylvania? That's not surprising. Nowadays the countryside in Pennsylvania is covered in greenery, but 430 million years ago the tallest plants around would have been knee-high to a grasshopper, had there been any grasshoppers. There weren't. Instead there were some small millipedes and other bugs crawling around under equally tiny plants. There were moss relatives a few inches tall, lichens on the rocks, and slimy mats of algae and bacteria in the wetter spots. Mostly though, it was just rocks, rocks, and more rocks, with some gravel, sand, and silt thrown in for good measure.

FOREST? HA, HA, HA. TREES HAVEN'T EVOLVED YET. IT LOOKS LIKE A FOREST TO YOU 'CAUSE YOU'RE THE SIZE OF A PINHEAD.

AH, I DO LOVE THE FOREST!

Robin Mite and Friar Millipede stroll through Sherwood Moss Patch.

LOVELY, LIVELY SEA LIFE

Now let's take a look at the oceans. What a contrast with the barren-looking landscape we just saw! Life in the oceans was in high gear 430 million years ago.

A warm, shallow sea covered most of North America. In it, zillions of animals were busy eating algae, plankton, and one another.

In some places, such as what is now the Great Lakes region of the United States, reefs formed. Here's what Racine, Wisconsin, looked like back then.

GREAT SWIMMING WEATHER HERE IN WISCONSIN TODAY, FOLKS! WE'VE GOT A SUNNY 82° AND ALL THE PLANKTON YOU CAN EAT!

82°

86°

AND WHERE, YOU MAY ASK, WERE THE FISH?

MIRROR, MIRROR, IN THE SEA, WHY DO I LOOK SO TURNIPY?

Good question! Actually, fish did exist back then, but they were small and not very common, and they usually lived near the shore, not the reef. Fish were the first vertebrates, or animals with backbones. Fossil fish scales date back more than 500 million years. The earliest fish were basic, no-frills models. They had a tail but no top or side fins to help them steer properly, so they must have been fairly slow and clumsy. These ancient fish didn't even have jaws. They did have a mouth, which they used to eat very small bits of food.

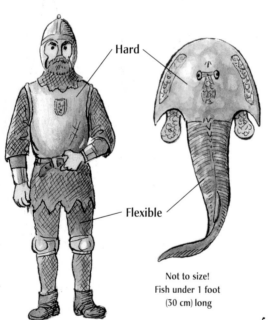

Hard

Flexible

Not to size!
Fish under 1 foot
(30 cm) long

Unlike modern vertebrates, most early fish had more bones on the outside than on the inside, forming an armored box around them. Jawless fish had their heyday in the period of time called the Silurian. In the following period, the Devonian, fish with jaws gradually took over.

Only two kinds of jawless fish are still alive today: lampreys and hagfishes. Both look very different from their Silurian ancestors. Lampreys suck blood from living fish, and hagfishes are deep-water scavengers and worm-eaters. Hagfishes secrete gobs of sticky mucus when bothered, and their table manners consist of climbing into dead or dying fish and eating them from the inside out. Dee-lightful!

A hagfish, curled up on the seafloor

Jawless Fish Sampler

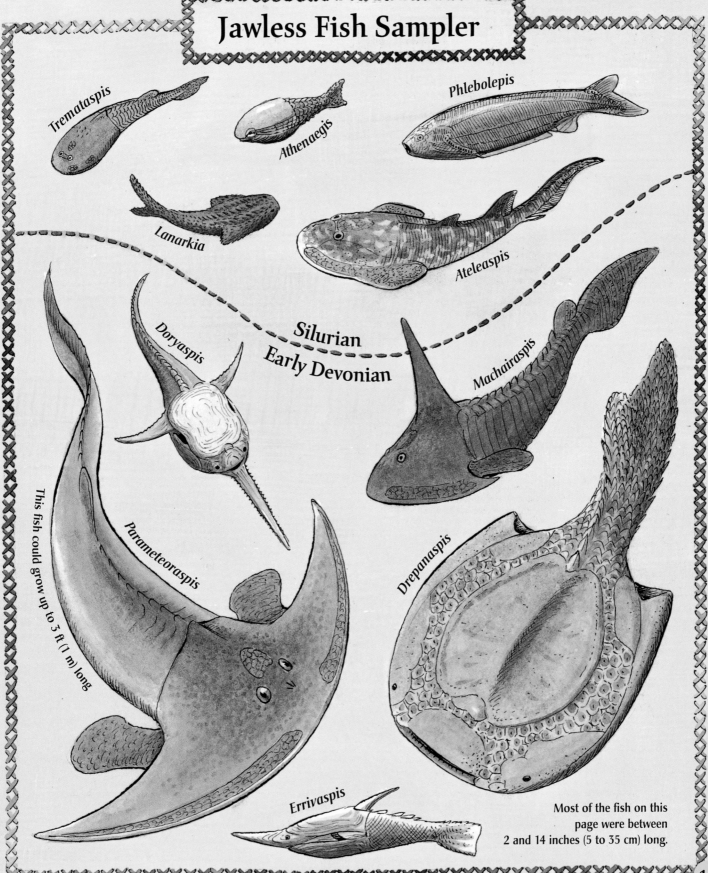

Tremataspis

Athenaegis

Phlebolepis

Lanarkia

Ateleaspis

Doryaspis

Silurian
Early Devonian

Machairaspis

This fish could grow up to 3 ft (1 m) long

Parameteoraspis

Drepanaspis

Errivaspis

Most of the fish on this page were between 2 and 14 inches (5 to 35 cm) long.

THE SILURIAN PLANET

In the 19th century, a British scientist by the name of Murchison found many fossils in Wales that seemed to belong to the same prehistoric time period. He called this period the Silurian after the Silures, a fierce Celtic tribe that lived in Wales in Roman times. Of course, there were no Romans, Silures, or anyone else around 430 million years ago. Instead, Wales was underwater, just like Wisconsin.

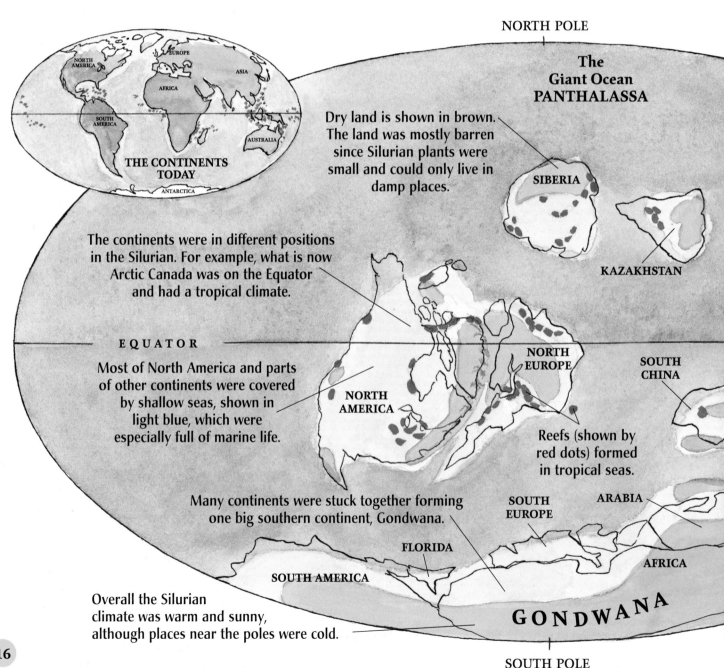

NORTH POLE

THE CONTINENTS TODAY

The
Giant Ocean
PANTHALASSA

Dry land is shown in brown. The land was mostly barren since Silurian plants were small and could only live in damp places.

SIBERIA

KAZAKHSTAN

The continents were in different positions in the Silurian. For example, what is now Arctic Canada was on the Equator and had a tropical climate.

EQUATOR

Most of North America and parts of other continents were covered by shallow seas, shown in light blue, which were especially full of marine life.

NORTH AMERICA

NORTH EUROPE

SOUTH CHINA

Reefs (shown by red dots) formed in tropical seas.

Many continents were stuck together forming one big southern continent, Gondwana.

SOUTH EUROPE

ARABIA

FLORIDA

AFRICA

SOUTH AMERICA

Overall the Silurian climate was warm and sunny, although places near the poles were cold.

GONDWANA

SOUTH POLE

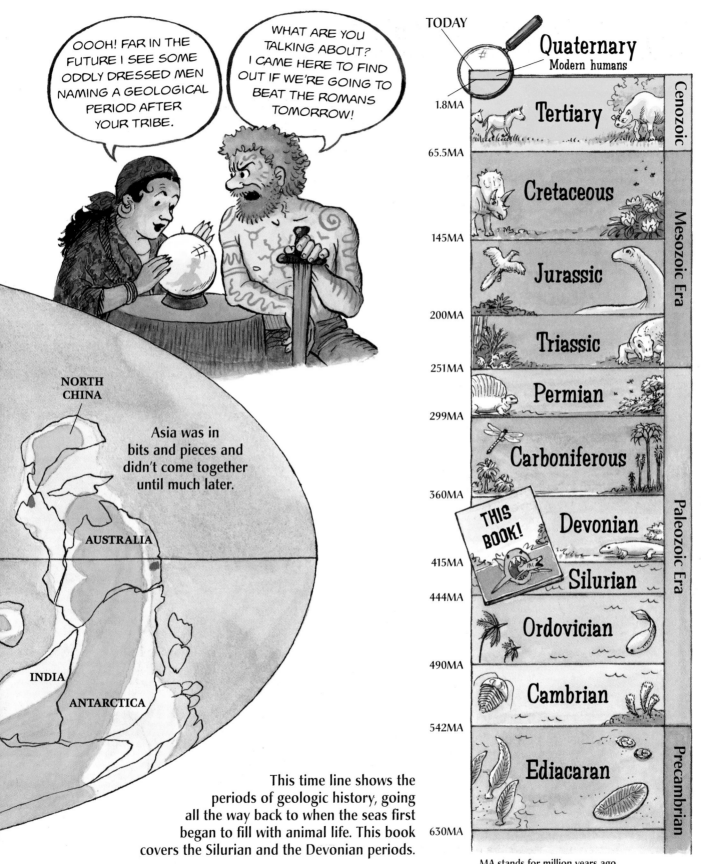

This time line shows the periods of geologic history, going all the way back to when the seas first began to fill with animal life. This book covers the Silurian and the Devonian periods.

MA stands for million years ago.
(In Latin, "million years" is "mega annum.")

LAND HO!

Why were there so few plants in the Silurian? Why were plants so slow to take advantage of all that empty real estate? The reason is that dry land is a harsh environment for life-forms used to soaking in a bath all day. It's no coincidence that life began in the oceans. Water keeps living things moist, protects them from too much ultraviolet radiation from the sun, and brings food and gases directly to their cellular doorstep.

WE WANT OUR MONEY BACK! THAT CRUISE TO DRY LAND WAS AWFUL! WE SHRIVELED UP AFTER FIVE MINUTES OF SIGHTSEEING!

JUST LOOK AT MY HUSBAND! IT WILL TAKE WEEKS OF SOAKING TO PLUMP HIM BACK UP!

7 SEAS CRUISE

SEE WEED TRAVEL

Recipe #1 How to Make a Land Plant

MAIN INGREDIENT: Freshwater green algae

1. Take some freshwater algae and cover it in a waterproof wrapper, called cuticle, so it won't dry out.

2. Make little holes in the cuticle to let air in and out. Remember, plants need to breathe!

Close-up of cuticle. The holes are called stomata.

WHEEE!

CALIFORNIA OR BUST!

3. Put a weatherproof coating on the plant's spores so they can travel through air instead of water. Spores are tiny packets of genetic material for making a new plant. They are smaller and simpler than seeds, which evolved later.

4. If you want your plant to get bigger, you'll have to put in little pipes so it can suck up water from the ground and bring it to the rest of the plant.

The very first plants had no plumbing. They were related to modern liverworts and mosses.

Plants probably got their start when some freshwater algae figured out how not to become toast every time the pond they lived in dried up. We don't know when this first happened. The oldest fossils of actual bits of plant are from the early Silurian, but scientists have found fossil plant spores that are much older.

Actually, the very first colonizers of land might not have been plants at all, but lichens, which are a partnership between an alga and a fungus. To this day lichens like to make their home on bare rocks, something there were plenty of in the Silurian. Lichens may have paved the way for plants by putting a first thin crust of living matter on the landscape.

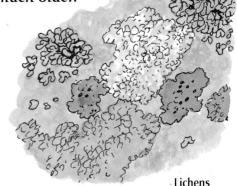

Lichens

As soon as there were enough plants, fungi, and other goodies on land to provide some food, animals crawled out of the water to join the fun. The oldest land animal fossils are of arthropods.

Recipe #2 How to Make a Land Animal

MAIN INGREDIENT:
An aquatic arthropod
(an animal with a jointed shell)

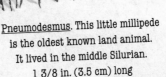
BUG WAX
PROTECTS! ADDS SHINE!

2. Put a waxy coating on the shell to keep the bug from drying out.

3. Bugs need to breathe, too! Make little holes in the shell to let air into tubes called tracheae, which will take the air to the rest of the animal's body.

1. Strengthen the arthropod's shell and muscles so that the animal can walk around easily on land, where everything weighs much more than in the water.

Pneumodesmus. This little millipede is the oldest known land animal. It lived in the middle Silurian.
1 3/8 in. (3.5 cm) long

Breathing holes, called spiracles

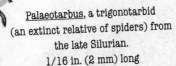

Palaeotarbus, a trigonotarbid (an extinct relative of spiders) from the late Silurian.
1/16 in. (2 mm) long

Note: this is just one of several possible recipes for making a land animal. You'll need quite a different recipe if you want to make a worm or four-legged animal!

GETTING GREENER

Plants kept a low profile in Silurian times, but all sorts of new plants took off in the beginning of the Devonian period. That's where we are now, on a warm, humid day in Quebec, Canada. Nowadays plants fight for space, but 400 million years ago there was still a lot of elbow room, and each plant could send out runners and spread out as much as it liked. The landscape looked like a giant patchwork quilt, with just one species of plant per patch.

Prototaxites

Prototaxites log

Pertica, at 3 ft (1 m) high, was the tallest plant around.

Sawdonia

Most of these plants were short, but you may have noticed some tall things looming in the distance. Scientists have found loglike fossils called *Prototaxites* up to 30 feet (8 meters) long. Trees didn't evolve until later in the Devonian, and parks with obelisks in them were a good 400 million years away, so what could these logs have been? One possibility is that they were mega-mushrooms, giant fungi that towered above the surrounding vegetation.

EEK! THERE'S A HUMONGOUS FUNGUS AMONG US!

...and Buggier

Scurrying around under the new plants were a number of new bugs. Centipedes, millipedes, mites, and trigonotarbids had been around since the Silurian. Now they were joined by springtails (six-legged relatives of insects), daddy longlegs, and the oldest known true insect, *Rhyniognatha*.

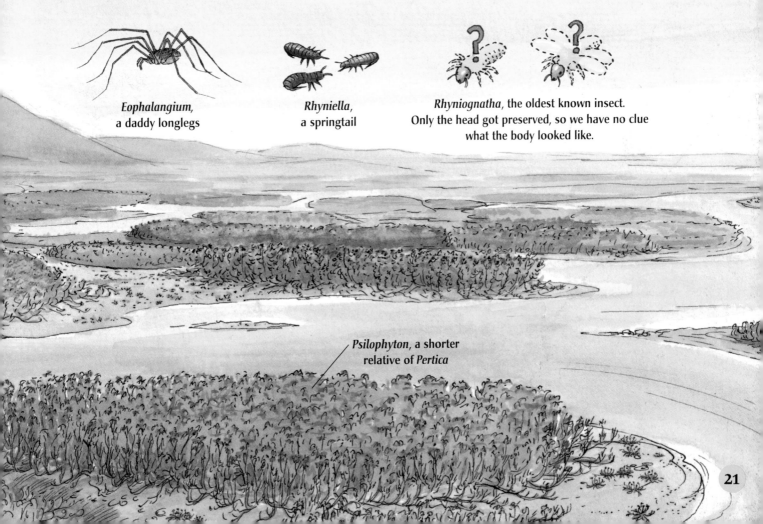

Eophalangium, a daddy longlegs

Rhyniella, a springtail

Rhyniognatha, the oldest known insect. Only the head got preserved, so we have no clue what the body looked like.

Psilophyton, a shorter relative of *Pertica*

THE BIRTH OF DIRT

Once plants had spread out sideways all they could, they began to bump into each other and to fight for light and for a good place to send out their spores. The result? They invented a stiff main trunk and shot upwards. They also developed primitive leaves to catch more light.

The plants we see here grew in New York State in the middle of the Devonian. By then there were big shrubs and even trees. Longer roots developed to anchor these larger plants and to collect enough water and minerals for them. Deeper roots and more plant matter meant that a significant amount of dirt—more correctly, soil—began to build up for the first time.

Eospermatopteris. There are many good fossils of the trunk, but we don't know what the top looked like, so this is just a guess.

Lepidosigillaria

Tetraxylopteris, an extinct relative of modern woody plants

Leclercqia

Leclercqia and *Lepidosigillaria* belonged to a group of plants called lycopods. Only a few small lycopods survive today.

We take soil for granted, but it barely existed before plants became common. Acids in plants help break bits of rock into smaller and smaller pieces, and these mix with organic matter (dead plants and the fungi, bacteria, and animals that help them fall apart) to form soil. Soil in turn supports more happy plants, which help create more soil, and so on toward an ever greener planet.

NO DIRT? HOW DID THEY MANAGE?

Bigger, Better Bugs

Bugs in the meantime had also gotten bigger and more varied. Spiders and centipedes crawled around under the new, improved plants searching for fellow bugs to eat. The rest of the bugs all ate rotting plant matter. Most bugs still hadn't figured out how to eat fresh plants, which are hard to digest. Instead they had to wait for bacteria and fungi in the soil to have a go at the plants first. Among these eaters of leftovers were millipedes, mites, worms (we assume—as usual, they didn't fossilize), and springtails.

ROTTEN SALAD BAR

SPORE TOPPING

FUNGUS DRESSING

Freshwater habitats had more life in them, thanks to nutrients from all the plants on the land around them.

THE DEVONIAN PLANET

The Devonian period got its name from Devonshire, in the south of England, where rocks and fossils from this period were first studied. The Devonian, which began around 415 million years ago, lasted for 55 million years. That's twice as long as the Silurian.

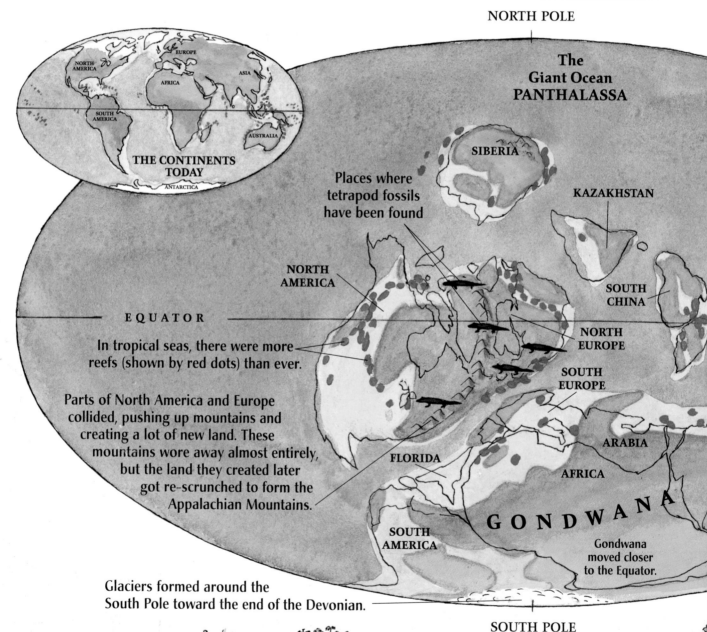

NORTH POLE

The Giant Ocean PANTHALASSA

THE CONTINENTS TODAY

NORTH AMERICA · EUROPE · ASIA · AFRICA · SOUTH AMERICA · AUSTRALIA · ANTARCTICA

SIBERIA

KAZAKHSTAN

Places where tetrapod fossils have been found

NORTH AMERICA

SOUTH CHINA

EQUATOR

In tropical seas, there were more reefs (shown by red dots) than ever.

NORTH EUROPE

SOUTH EUROPE

Parts of North America and Europe collided, pushing up mountains and creating a lot of new land. These mountains wore away almost entirely, but the land they created later got re-scrunched to form the Appalachian Mountains.

ARABIA

FLORIDA

AFRICA

SOUTH AMERICA

G O N D W A N A

Gondwana moved closer to the Equator.

Glaciers formed around the South Pole toward the end of the Devonian.

SOUTH POLE

Early Devonian

A lot happened in the Devonian. Fish became major players for the first time. They became so common and diverse in both fresh and salt water that the Devonian is sometimes referred to as the Age of Fishes.

On land, a green revolution took place that changed the planet forever. The vegetation went from ankle-high plants to full-fledged forests inhabited by all sorts of bugs...and us! OK, not us exactly, but our distant ancestors, the first tetrapods, or four-legged animals. "Tetrapod" means "four-footed" in Greek.

AFTER MANY MILLIONS OF YEARS OF WARM WEATHER, WE'RE IN FOR A COLD SNAP, SO PLEASE BUNDLE UP!

As the Devonian came to a close, a series of extinctions hit warm-water marine life especially hard. The culprit? Some scientists think it was plants! Plants back then may have taken in so much carbon dioxide—the greenhouse gas that keeps our planet warm—that they caused a spell of global cooling. (Nowadays we have too much carbon dioxide in the air, and it is causing global warming.) It seems that the cold temperatures were one of the reasons that many warm-water creatures died off, including most of the lovely reef-builders. It took a long time for reefs to recover.

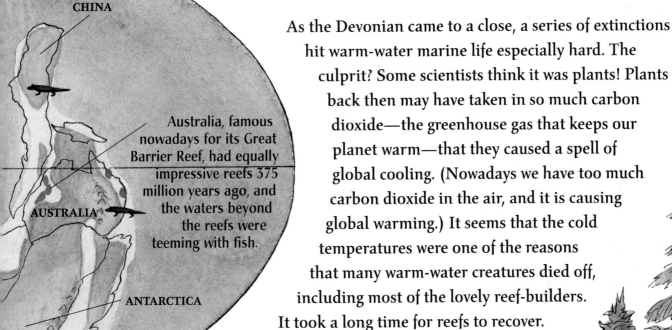

NORTH CHINA

Australia, famous nowadays for its Great Barrier Reef, had equally impressive reefs 375 million years ago, and the waters beyond the reefs were teeming with fish.

AUSTRALIA

ANTARCTICA

Middle Devonian

Late Devonian

FISHY NEWS

The big news in the fish world had to do with jaws. Fish came up with jaws in the late Ordovician, although jaws didn't become common until much later, in the Devonian. All sorts of new fish evolved as a result. Jaws turned out to be a most versatile tool. They allowed fish to say good-bye to a monotonous diet of teensy stuff. Now fish could grab, slice, and dice to their heart's content. They could even eat one another, and they did so with great gusto. In many environments, fish became top predators, usurping this honor from the eurypterids. Vertebrates—fish and their four-legged descendants— have kept the title of top predator ever since, both in the water and on land.

The Devonian Herald

October 20th, 405 MA

"JAWS" TAKE OVER
ORDOVICIAN INVENTION CATCHES ON BIG TIME IN THE DEVONIAN

Dr. Akanth, of the University of Southern Gondwana, gave a demonstration last night of how the new body part works. It consists of two sections, an upper and a lower jaw. Each jaw is normally lined with rows of hard pointy things called teeth. Dr. Akanth, who has jaws herself, cannot say enough good things about them. "My biggest fear is that I'll become fat because I can eat so many more things than I could before," she said. Dr. Akanth predicts that it won't be long before most fish have jaws.

LOCAL NEWS – Three Teenage Placoderms Rescued from Drying Pond

The three East Gondwana residents had been ... small pond when the water level ...

THE GREAT DEVONIAN FISH RACE

At the beginning of the Devonian, four groups of fish with jaws—acanthodians, placoderms, sharks, and bony fish—took off in a race to see who would become most common and diverse. Jawless fish were still around, mucking around on the bottom beneath their jawed cousins, but they became less and less common. By the end of the Devonian they had petered out almost entirely.

GET READY, GET SET...

① ACANTHODIANS

Acanthodians were distinguished by having a spine in front of each fin—a prickly mouthful for anyone trying to eat them, for sure. The acanthodians got off to an early start; their fossilized fin spines go as far back as the Ordovician period. In fact, they may have been the first fish with jaws. They kept a steady pace through the Devonian and beyond, only to finally go extinct in the Permian.

Climatius, from Britain, 5 1/2 in. (14 cm)

Parexus, a super-spiny acanthodian, also from Britain; a little over 6 in. (16 cm) long

Howittacanthus lived in Australia. It swam with its mouth open to filter plankton, much the way modern-day anchovies do. 10 in. (25 cm)

② PLACODERMS

The placoderms were the group of fish that grew the fastest at the beginning of the Devonian, with many new species cropping up. Placoderms had an armored head and trunk, often with a hinge between the two parts that allowed the mouth to open wider.

Placoderms were generally on the small side, but they did produce some giants such as *Dunkleosteus*, the terror of late Devonian seas. *Dunkleosteus* could be up to 20 feet (6 m) long. It had big, razor-sharp ridges of bone instead of individual teeth.

Dunkleosteus is seen chasing a small shark.
20 ft (6 m) long

The most common placoderm of all was the bug-eyed *Bothriolepis*. This fish had crablike front fins and eyes that stuck up out of holes in the head armor.

Were you hoping to buy a placoderm for your aquarium? Sorry! After being top fish for millions of years, placoderms faded out at the end of the Devonian, never to be seen again.

Bothriolepis, about 1 foot (30 cm) long

The first sharks appeared as far back as the Ordovician, but we don't know what they looked like because all they left behind were microscopic pointy scales. Could the earliest sharks have been toothless? We don't know! The first fossil shark teeth are from the early Devonian. Like sharks today, Devonian sharks replaced old teeth with new ones throughout their lifetime. Devonian sharks did so fairly slowly, but later sharks shed teeth with such abandon that shark teeth became the most common vertebrate fossils in the world.

Cladoselache lived in
North America in the late Devonian.
About 4 ft (1.2 m)

A small bony fish is about to become *Cladoselache*'s lunch. *Cladoselache* in turn probably had to avoid becoming lunch for giant placoderms such as *Dunkleosteus*.

The mouth of early sharks was at the front of the head. In modern sharks it is below.

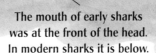

Fossils of whole sharks, on the other hand, are extremely rare. Sharks and their relatives are known as cartilaginous fish because their skeleton is made entirely of cartilage rather than bone. Cartilage is softer than bone and usually falls apart before it can fossilize.

Assorted Devonian shark teeth.
Scientists can tell prehistoric sharks apart by their teeth.

AS WE APPROACH THE FINISH LINE, THE SHARKS ARE KEEPING A STEADY PACE, BUT THE PLACODERMS ARE LOSING STEAM!

Bony fish account for 96 percent of all fish alive today, from minnows to tuna, electric eels, and colorful coral reef fish. Their humble beginnings consist of a few scales and teeth from the Silurian, but like the other contestants in this race, bony fish really got going in the Devonian. Some special features of bony fish are a skeleton made of true bone (as opposed to cartilage in sharks), overlapping scales, and, surprisingly, a lung in addition to their gills. In most bony fish alive today, the lung has turned into a swim bladder. This is a bag of gas that keeps the fish from sinking.

Early in the Devonian, the bony fish split into two big groups, the ray-fins and the lobe-fins. They are distinguished by— surprise, surprise!—the structure of their fins.

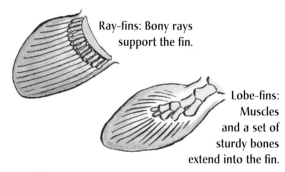

Ray-fins: Bony rays support the fin.

Lobe-fins: Muscles and a set of sturdy bones extend into the fin.

Mimia, a common little ray-fin from Australia, up to 8 in. (20 cm) long

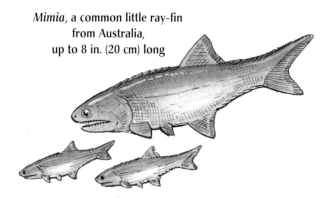

Ray-fins

These are what we think of as "regular fish." The vast majority of living fish are ray-fins, but in the Devonian their numbers were more modest.

These fish all lived in eastern Canada in the late Devonian.

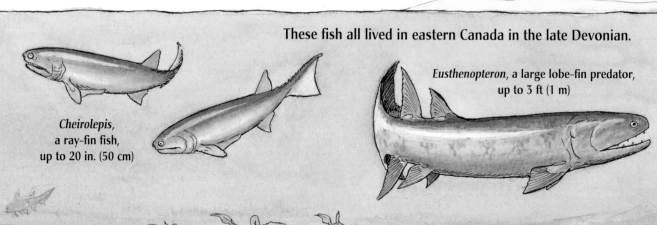

Cheirolepis, a ray-fin fish, up to 20 in. (50 cm)

Eusthenopteron, a large lobe-fin predator, up to 3 ft (1 m)

Lobe-fins

Lobe-fins did very well in the Devonian, better even than their ray-fin relatives. Many of the larger lobe-fins became top predators, especially in freshwater environments. Nowadays the only surviving lobe-fins are three kinds of lungfishes and a single kind of coelacanth (pronounced SEE-luh-canth), a fish that was thought to have become extinct along with the dinosaurs but which turned up alive in the 1930s in the Indian Ocean. These surviving lobe-fins are our closest living fish relatives.

The Winners

Our direct ancestors, though, were neither lungfishes nor coelacanths. We descend from another branch on the lobe-fin family tree, one that gave rise to all four-legged animals, or tetrapods. Although the fishes in this group eventually became extinct, their descendants are alive and well in the form of every single amphibian, reptile, bird, and mammal on the planet. Throw in the ray-fins as well, and we see that Devonian bony fish are the ancestors of all living vertebrates except for sharks and their kin, lampreys, and hagfishes. Bony fish definitely get first prize!

BONY FISH HAVE WON THE GOLD! SHARKS ARE IN SECOND PLACE.

FIRST PLACE

SECOND PLACE

Elpistostege, a very close relative of tetrapods, up to 5 ft (1.5 m)

Miguashaia, an oddly shaped coelacanth, up to 18 in. (45 cm)

Scaumenacia, a lungfish, up to 24 in. (60 cm)

THE FIRST FORESTS

Meanwhile, back on land, a tree called *Archaeopteris* (not to be confused with the Jurassic bird *Archaeopteryx*) created the world's first real forests. *Archaeopteris* had deep roots and a solid wood trunk very much like that of a pine tree. Its leaves, on the other hand, looked fernlike. And like a fern, *Archeopteris* reproduced by means of spores—a strange hodgepodge indeed! Hodgepodge or not, it was wildly successful for much of the late Devonian. It grew from the tropics all the way to fairly cool regions. Like all spore plants, it always stuck fairly close to water, since spore plants need moisture in order to reproduce.

Archaeopteris won the fight for light, hands down. Not only was it taller than the competition, it also had improved leaves that created a denser shade.

Archaeopteris

TRY GROWING THROUGH THAT, SUCKER!

And in case that wasn't enough, it shed its branches from time to time, smothering whatever was trying to sprout below it. Forest soils became especially thick and moist thanks to the shade, the leaf litter, and the longer roots holding everything in place.

Seeds of Change

After being so successful, Archaeopteris dwindled and finally disappeared right near the end of the Devonian. Nobody knows why. The future, in any case, belonged to the new kids on the block: plants that made seeds. All the plants we have seen so far were spore plants, like our living ferns and mosses. In the Devonian, some plants gradually went from making spores to making seeds. These new seed plants were able to grow in all sorts of different environments, including places that were too harsh or dry for spore plants.

Rhacophyton, a fern relative

Elkinsia, one of the first seed plants

APPENDIX I: A TIME LINE OF LIFE ON EARTH

Look! My appendix got taken out!

They don't mean THAT kind, silly!

The Earth forms along with the rest of the solar system.

4.5 BILLION YEARS AGO

The Earth is still very hot. It is bombarded by leftover bits and pieces of solar system.

The Earth has cooled. Water vapor rains down for millions of years and fills the oceans.

4 BILLION YEARS AGO

FIRST LIFE OF SOME SORT

The seawater is loaded with minerals that are the building blocks of big molecules and eventually of life. It is sometimes referred to as the

Primordial Soup.

If we traveled this far back, we would die, because the air has no free oxygen in it for us to breathe.

3.5 BILLION YEARS AGO

Tiny fossils that may be bacteria (single cells with no nucleus) have been found from this time.

Early life-forms —probably bacteria— begin to photosynthesize, meaning they use sunlight to make food. This releases oxygen into the water.

O_2 BURP!

3 BILLION YEARS AGO

2.5 BILLION YEARS AGO

Cyanobacteria keep pumping oxygen into the oceans. As a result, iron in the seawater rusts and falls to the bottom.

Photosynthetic bacteria called cyanobacteria form rocky mounds called stromatolites.

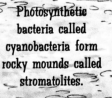

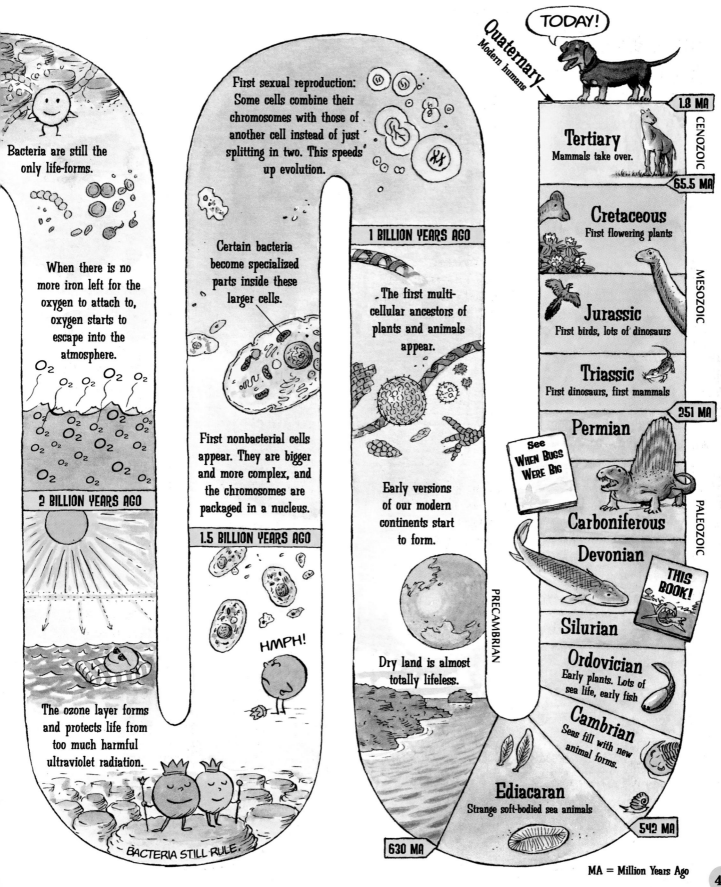

Bacteria are still the only life-forms.

When there is no more iron left for the oxygen to attach to, oxygen starts to escape into the atmosphere.

O_2 O_2 O_2 O_2 O_2 O_2 O_2 O_2 O_2 O_2 O_2 O_2 O_2 O_2 O_2 O_2 O_2 O_2 O_2 O_2 O_2

2 BILLION YEARS AGO

The ozone layer forms and protects life from too much harmful ultraviolet radiation.

BACTERIA STILL RULE.

First sexual reproduction: Some cells combine their chromosomes with those of another cell instead of just splitting in two. This speeds up evolution.

Certain bacteria become specialized parts inside these larger cells.

First nonbacterial cells appear. They are bigger and more complex, and the chromosomes are packaged in a nucleus.

1.5 BILLION YEARS AGO

HMPH!

1 BILLION YEARS AGO

The first multi-cellular ancestors of plants and animals appear.

Early versions of our modern continents start to form.

Dry land is almost totally lifeless.

630 MA

PRECAMBRIAN

Quaternary
Modern humans

TODAY!

1.8 MA

CENOZOIC

Tertiary
Mammals take over.

65.5 MA

Cretaceous
First flowering plants

MESOZOIC

Jurassic
First birds, lots of dinosaurs

Triassic
First dinosaurs, first mammals

251 MA

Permian

See WHEN BUGS WERE BIG

Carboniferous

PALEOZOIC

Devonian

THIS BOOK!

Silurian

Ordovician
Early plants. Lots of sea life, early fish

Cambrian
Seas fill with new animal forms.

Ediacaran
Strange soft-bodied sea animals

542 MA

MA = Million Years Ago

Appendix II: A Chart to Help Keep the Vertebrates Straight

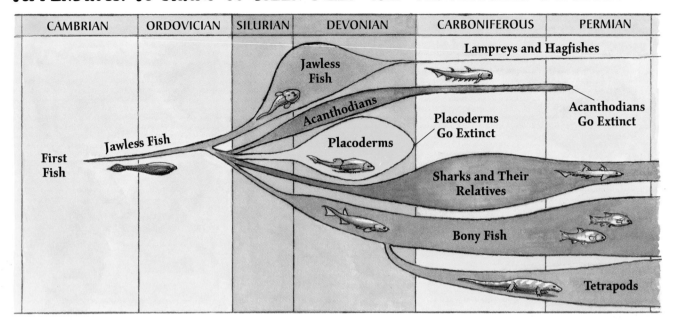

CAMBRIAN	ORDOVICIAN	SILURIAN	DEVONIAN	CARBONIFEROUS	PERMIAN

Jawless Fish

Lampreys and Hagfishes

First Fish

Jawless Fish

Acanthodians

Placoderms

Placoderms Go Extinct

Acanthodians Go Extinct

Sharks and Their Relatives

Bony Fish

Tetrapods

Where to Learn More

The three best places to learn more about the middle Paleozoic and its inhabitants are libraries, natural history museums, and the Web.

If you go to the library, you probably won't find any books just about the Paleozoic, at least not in the children's or young adult section, so be sure to browse in the adult science section as well. A number of books about dinosaurs start out with chapters about what came before. One example is *The Concise Dinosaur Encyclopedia*, by David Burnie and artist John Sibbick. Also look out for books about the history of life, since they will include sections on the Silurian and Devonian, for instance *Prehistoric Journey*, by Kirk Johnson and Richard Stucky of the Denver Museum of Natural History.

One of the very few items that your local library may carry that is specifically about life before the dinosaurs is a BBC video called *Walking with Monsters*. It's great fun to watch, but take the science in it with a grain of salt. The folks who created it made up *lots* of the details. For instance, they show exactly what the mating ritual of a tetrapod called *Hynerpeton* was like. That's fine, except that the only fossils of *Hynerpeton* that have been found so far are some shoulder and jaw bones. Scientists don't even know what the complete animal looked like, much less what its dating preferences were!

Curious to check out what *is* known about *Hynerpeton*? Try the Internet. You should be able to consult it at your local library if you don't have Internet access at home. The absolute best site for learning about life on land and in freshwater in the Devonian is called Devonian Times, www.devoniantimes.org. It has all sorts of in-depth information that you won't easily find anywhere else, and good links to related sites. You will definitely get the lowdown on *Hynerpeton* there. For a funny, wacky site, check out artist Ray Troll's site, www.trollart.com. You'll find a good page on *Tiktaalik*, and a link to a song. More serious sites are Tree of Life,

www.tolweb.org, which covers both living and extinct life-forms, and Palaeos, www.palaeos.com, which is specifically about prehistoric life. Both can get pretty technical, but if you don't let yourself be daunted by the scientific language, you are likely to find what you are looking for. For maps of the prehistoric world, go to www.scotese.com, click on Earth History, and then choose a time period. And if you want to take a swim in the Silurian, go to the Silurian Virtual Reef at http://www.mpm.edu/collections/learn/reef/.

Search engines such as Google or Yahoo turn up a wealth of information. Image searches are the most fun. Choose the "images" option, then type in the name of any creature, and you'll get some photos of fossils. With luck, you'll get some reconstructions as well. Try *Ichthyostega*, for instance, and you'll get hundreds of images—even an *Ichthyostega* made out of origami! I've included a few very obscure characters in this book that won't get you any hits, but they are the exception. Please remember that anyone can set up a Web site, so not everything you will encounter will be good science. That's one reason it's good to follow links from reliable sites like the ones I've mentioned above.

The web ties in with the other great resource, natural history museums. Visit one if you can, but if you aren't lucky enough to live near one, you can consult their Web sites to find out what's in them. Some of the museum sites, such the Berkeley Museum of Natural History (www.ucmp.berkeley.edu), include a lot of extra information and can be a good source if you are writing a report or simply want to learn more.

Note: New information appears all the time, so this book is up to date as of now, but in a few years some of the facts will have changed. Science isn't static. The discovery of *Tiktaalik*, for instance, was announced when I'd already done sketches. I had to rework the last section of the book to include it!

HOW TO PRONOUNCE THE SCIENTIFIC TERMS IN THIS BOOK

Acanthodian (AH-kan-THOE-dee-an)

Amblypigid (Am-blee-PIH-jid)

Amphicyrtoceras (AM-fee-SIR-to-ser-us)

Archaeopteris (AR-kee-OP-te-ris)

Archaeopteryx (AR-kee-OP-te-ricks)

Arthropod (AR-thro-pod)

Ateleaspis (uh-TEE-lee-ASS-pis)

Athenaegis (ath-en-EE-jis)

Bothriolepis (BAH-three-oh-LEE-pis)

Brachiopod (BRAK-ee-oh-pod)

Bryozoan (BRY-uh-ZO-an)

Cambrian (KAM-bree-an)

Canis (KAY-nus)

Carboniferous (kar-bon-IF-er-us)

Carcinosoma (KAR-sin-oh-SOH-ma)

Cenozoic (sen-oh-ZO-ik)

Cheirolepis (ky-roe-LEE-pis)

Cladoselache (klay-doe-SEL-uh-kee)

Climatius (kly-MAT-ee-us)

Cretaceous (kre-TAY-shus)

Crinoid (KRY-noid)

Cuticle (CUE-tik-ul)

Cystoid (SISS-toid)

Dawsonoceras (DAW-sun-oh-SER-us)

Devonian (de-VONE-ee-an)

Doryaspis (dor-ee-ASS-pis)

Drepanaspis (drep-uh-NASS-pis)

Dunkleosteus (dun-klee-AW-stee-us)

Ediacaran (EE-dee-AK-ar-un)

Elkinsia (el-KIN-see-uh)

Elpistostege (el-pis-toe-STEE-ghee)

Eophalangium (ee-oh-fa-LAN-gee-um)

Eospermatopteris
  (EE-oh-sper-ma-TOP-ter-is)

Errivaspis (air-ih-VASS-pis)

Eurypterid (yer-IP-ter-id)

Eusthenopteron (yoos-then-OP-ter-on)

Fungi (FUN-guy or FUNJ-eye)

Gondwana (gon-DWON-ah)

Graptolite (GRAP-toe-lite)

Howittacanthus (how-it-uh-KAN-thus)

Ichthyostega (ik-thee-oh-STEE-guh)

Jurassic (jur-ASS-ik)

Lanarkia (la-NAR-kee-ah)

Leclercqia (le-KLER-kee-ah)

Lepidosigillaria
  (lep-id-oh-si-jill-AHR-ee-ah)

Lichen (LY-kun)

Liverworts (LI-ver-werts)

Machairaspis (mac-eye-RASS-pis)

Mesozoic (meh-zuh-ZO-ik)

Miguashaia (mig-wa-SHY-ah)

Mimia (MIM-ee-ah)

Nautiloid (NAWT-uh-loid)

Ordovician (or-do-VISH-ee-an)

Palaeotarbus (pay-lee-oh-TAR-bus)

Paleozoic (pay-lee-oh-ZO-ik)

Panthalassa (pan-thal-AH-suh)

Parameteoraspis
  (pair-uh-MEE-tee-oh-RASS-pis)

Parexus (pa-REX-us)

Permian (PURR-mee-an)

Pertica (PURR-tik-uh)

Phlebolepis (fleb-oh-LEE-pis)

Placoderm (PLAK-oh-derm)

Pneumodesmus (new-mo-DES-mus)

Prototaxites (PRO-toe-tax-EYE-tees)

Pseudoscorpion (sue-doe-SKOR-pee-un)

Psilophyton (si-lo-FIE-tun)

Pterygotus (TER-ih-GO-tus)

Quaternary (KWA-ter-nair-ee)

Rhacophyton (rak-o-FIE-ton)

Rhyniella (rye-nee-EL-uh)

Rhyniognatha (rye-nee-ohg-NATH-uh)

Sawdonia (saw-DOE-nee-uh)

Scaumenacia (skow-men-AY-see-uh)

Silurian (si-LURE-ee-an)

Stomata (stoe-MAH-tuh)

Stromatoporoid (stroe-muh-TOP-uh-roid)

Tertiary (TER-shee-air-ee)

Tetraxilopteris (teh-truh-zie-LOP-ter-is)

Tiktaalik (tick-TA-lik)

Tracheae (TRAY-kee-uh)

Tremataspis (trem-ah-TASS-pis)

Triassic (try-ASS-ik)

Trigonotarbid (trig-oh-no-TAR-bid)

Trilobite (TRY-lo-bite)

GLOSSARY OF WORDS NOT DEFINED IN THE TEXT

Bacteria: Microscopic single-cell life-forms with a distinctive kind of cell wall and no nucleus.

Bug: In this book bug is used in the popular sense to mean insects as well as other terrestrial invertebrates such as spiders, centipedes, worms, and the like.

Chromosomes: Tiny strands inside a cell that contain information for making a new cell.

Fossil: Remains or traces of a living being that over millions of years have turned into stone.

Fungi (singular: fungus): The group that includes mushrooms, yeast, and molds.

Fungi do not photosynthesize and cannot make their own food from scratch as plants can. Instead, they recycle nutrients created by plants and other life-forms.

Invertebrate: An animal without a backbone.

Nucleus: A little rounded "bag" inside most cells that contains the chromosomes.

Nutrients: Substances such as minerals, vitamins, and sugars, that living beings use to stay alive and grow.

Ozone layer: A layer of ozone (O_3, a form of oxygen with a strong odor) surrounding the Earth 10 to 12 miles above its surface.

Plankton: Tiny animals and other life-forms that drift in the water and are a source of food for many larger animals.

Predator: An animal that hunts other animals for food.

Scavenger: An animal that eats the remains of dead animals that it finds.

Ultraviolet radiation: Also known as UV light, it is a form of light that we can't see but that causes sunburn.

Vertebrate: An animal with a backbone.

Index

Author's Sources for Text and Images

Books

Barnes, Robert D. *Invertebrate Zoology.* Fort Worth, TX: Harcourt Brace College Publishers, 1991.

Behrensmeyer, Anna K., et al., eds. *Terrestrial Ecosystems Throughout Time.* Chicago: University of Chicago Press, 1992.

Caroll, Robert L. *Vertebrate Paleontology and Evolution.* New York: W.H. Freeman and Co., 1997.

Clack, Jennifer. *Gaining Ground.* Bloomington, IN: Indiana University Press, 2002.

Clarkson, E. N. K. *Invertebrate Paleontology and Evolution.* Oxford: Blackwell Science, 1998.

Fortey, Richard. *Life.* New York: Vintage Books, 1999.

Gensel, Patricia G., and Dianne Edwards, eds. *Plants Invade the Land.* New York: Columbia University Press, 2001.

Janvier, Phillippe. *Early Vertebrates.* New York: Oxford University Press, 2003.

Johnson, Kirk R., and Richard K. Stuckey. *Prehistoric Journey.* Boulder, CO: Denver Museum of Natural History/Roberts Rinehart Publishers, 1995.

Kenrick, Paul, and Paul Davis. *Fossil Plants.* Washington: Smithsonian Books, 2004.

Long, John A. *The Rise of Fishes.* Baltimore: The Johns Hopkins University Press, 1995.

Maisey, John G. *Discovering Fossil Fishes.* Boulder, CO: Westview Press, 2000.

McKerrow, W. S., ed. *The Ecology of Fossils.* Cambridge, MA.: MIT Press, 1979.

Nardi, James B. *The World Beneath Our Feet: A Guide to Life in the Soil.* New York: Oxford University Press, 2003.

Schultze, Hans-Peter, and Richard Cloutier, eds. *Devonian Fishes and Plants of Miguasha, Quebec, Canada.* Munich: Verlag Dr. Friedrich Pfeil, 1996.

Stewart, Wilson N., and Gar W. Rothwell. *Paleobotany and the Evolution of Plants.* Cambridge: Cambridge University Press, 1993.

Wicander, Reed, and James S. Monroe. *Historical Geology: Evolution of Earth and Life Through Time.* Belmont, CA: Brooks/Cole–Thomson, 2004.

Wood, Rachel. *Reef Evolution.* New York: Oxford University Press, 1999.

Articles

Ahlberg, Per Erik, Jennifer A. Clack, and Henning Blom. 2005. "The axial skeleton of the Devonian tetrapod *Ichthyostega.*" *Nature,* 437(1): 137–140.

Anderson, L. I., and N. H. Trewin. 2003. "An Early Devonian arthropod fauna from the Windyfield Cherts, Aberdeenshire, Scotland." *Palaeontology,* 46(3): 467–509.

Briggs, Derek E.G., and Richard A. Fortey. 2005. "Wonderful strife: systematics, stem groups, and the phylogenetic signal of the Cambrian radiation." *Paleobiology,* 31 (2, Supplement): 94–112.

Clack, Jennifer A. "Getting a leg up on land." *Scientific American* (December 2005), 100–106.

Daeschler, Edward B., Neil H. Shubin, and Farish A. Jenkins, Jr. 2006. "A Devonian tetrapod-like fish and the evolution of the tetrapod body plan." *Nature,* 440(6): 757–763.

Dunlop, J. A., et. al. 2004. "A harvestman (Arachnida: Opiliones) from the Early Devonian Rhynie cherts, Aberdeenshire, Scotland." *Transactions of the Royal Society of Edinburgh: Earth Sciences,* 94: 341–354.

Engel, M. S., and Grimaldi, D. A. 2004. "New light shed on the oldest insect." *Nature,* 427: 627–630.

Griffing, David H., John S. Bridge, and Carol L. Hotton. 2004. "Coastal-fluvial palaeoenvironments and plant palaeoecology of the Lower Devonian (Emsian), Gaspé, Québec, Canada." *New Perspectives on the Old Red Sandstone.* Friend, P.F., and B.P.J. Williams, eds. London: Geological Society.

Hueber, Francis M. 2001. "Rotted wood-alga-fungus: the history and life of *Prototaxites* Dawson 1859." *Review of Palaeobotany and Palynology,* 116: 123–158.

Jahren, A. Hope, Steven Porter, and Jeffrey J. Kuglitsch. 2003. "Lichen metabolism identified in Early Devonian terrestrial organisms." *Geology,* 31(2): 99–102.

Jeram, A. J., P. A. Selden, and D. Edwards. 1990. "Land animals in the Silurian: arachnids and myriapods from Shropshire, England." *Science,* 250: 658–661.

Labandeira, Conrad C. 2005. "Invasion of the continents: cyanobacterial crusts to tree-inhabiting arthropods." *Trends in Ecology and Evolution,* 20(5): 253–262.

Pisani, Davide, Laura L. Poling, Maureen Lyons-Weiler, and S. Blair Hedges. 2004. "The colonization of land by animals: molecular phylogeny and divergence times among arthropods." *BMC Biolog,* 2:1.

Purnell, Mark A. 2002. "Feeding in extinct jawless heterostracan fishes and testing scenarios of early vertebrate evolution." *Proceedings of the Royal Society, London,* 269: 83–88.

Rose, Eben C., Nicola McLoughlin, and Martin D. Brasier. 2005. "Ground truth: the epistemology of searching for the earliest life on earth." *Life as we know it,* J. Seckbach, ed., vol 11: *Cellular Origin and Life in Extreme Habitats and Astrobiology,* Springer: 259-285.

Schubin, Neil H., Edward B. Daeschler, and Farish A. Jenkins, Jr. 2006. "The pectoral fin of *Tiktaalik roseae* and the origin of the tetrapod limb." *Nature,* 440(6): 764–771.

Selden, P. A., W. A. Shear, and P. M. Bonamo. 1991. "A spider and other arachnids from the Devonian of New York, and reinterpretations of Devonian Araneae." *Palaeontology,* 34:, 241–281.

Taggart, Ralph E., and Lee R. Parker. 1976. "A New Fossil Alga From the Silurian of Michigan." *American Journal of Botany,* 63(10): 1390–1392.

Wilson, H. M., and L. I. Anderson. 2004. "Morphology and taxonomy of Paleozoic millipedes (Diplopoda: Chilognatha: Archipolypoda) from Scotland." *Journal of Paleontology,* 78(1):169–184.

Web sites

A great many web sites were helpful in researching this book. A tiny sample:

The Silurian Virtual Reef, http://www.mpm.edu/collections/learn/reef/

Devonian Times, www.devoniantimes.org

The Rhynie Chert, http://www.abdn.ac.uk/rhynie/

Palaeos, www.palaeos.com

The Paleomap project, www.scotese.com and Ron Blakey's site http://jan.ucc.nau.edu/~rcb7/paleogeographic.html were the main sources for Paleomaps.

The International Comission on Stratigraphy, http://www.strati graphy.org/cheu.pdf is the source of the dates in the time lines.